SKYSCRAPERS!

Elizabeth Schmermund

Illustrated by Mike Crosier

Titles in the **Explore Engineering** Set

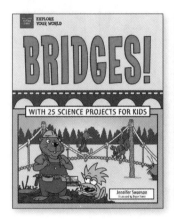

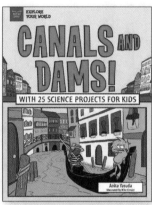

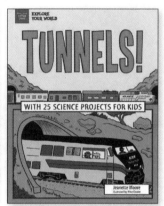

Check out more titles at www.nomadpress.net

Nomad Press
A division of Nomad Communications
10 9 8 7 6 5 4 3 2 1

This book was manufactured by Versa Press,
East Peoria, Illinois
August 2018, Job #J17-12601

ISBN Softcover: 978-1-61930-653-0
ISBN Hardcover: 978-1-61930-651-6

Educational Consultant, Marla Conn

Questions regarding the ordering of this book should be addressed to
Nomad Press
2456 Christian St.
White River Junction, VT 05001
www.nomadpress.net

Printed in the United States of America.

CONTENTS

Interested in primary sources? Look for this icon. Use a smartphone or tablet app to scan the QR code and explore more! Photos are also primary sources because a photograph takes a picture at the moment something happens.

If the QR code doesn't work, there's a list of URLs on the Resources page. Or, try searching the internet with the Keyword Prompts to find other helpful sources.

KEYWORD PROMPTS

skyscrapers 🔍

TIMELINE

1853:
American inventor Elisha Graves Otis develops an elevator with a safety device that keeps an elevator from falling down the shaft if the elevator cable breaks.

LATE 1800s:
Steel, instead of iron, starts to be used in buildings. The lower-weight steel allows much taller structures to be built.

JANUARY 4, 1885:
The world's first skyscraper is completed—the Home Insurance Building in Chicago, a 10-story, steel-framed building.

1889:
George A. Fuller builds the Tacoma Building using Bessemer steel beams. It is the first structure ever built in which the steel skeleton carries the load of the building, instead of the outside walls doing the job.

APRIL 22, 1931:
The Empire State Building is completed in New York City. At 1,250 feet, it will hold the title of world's tallest building for 40 years.

MARCH 12, 1930:
The Chrysler Building in New York City is completed, becoming the new world's tallest building for a short time.

AUGUST 15, 1895:
The American Surety Building is completed in New York City, becoming the world's tallest building. Architects begin to compete to build taller and grander buildings.

FEBRUARY 26, 1932:
The 285-foot-tall Flatiron Building in New York City is completed. It is one of the tallest buildings in the city and is one of the first buildings to use a steel framework.

2014:
Architect Stefano Boeri builds vertical forest skyscrapers in Milan, Italy.

APRIL 1973:
The World Trade Center towers are completed in New York, making them the world's tallest buildings. 1 World Trade Center is 1,355 feet tall and 2 World Trade Center is 1,348 feet tall.

JANUARY 2010:
The Burj Khalifa officially becomes the tallest building in the world at 2,722 feet and 160 stories.

SEPTEMBER 1973:
The Sears Tower (now called the Willis Tower) is completed in Chicago, surpassing the World Trade Center towers as the tallest building in the world. The tower is 1,450 feet tall, and is the first building to use the bundled tube construction method that soon becomes widely used in skyscraper design.

DECEMBER 31, 2004:
Taipei 101 in Taiwan becomes the tallest building in the world at 1,670 feet and 101 stories.

APRIL 13, 1998:
At 1,483 feet, the Petronas Towers in Malaysia officially become the tallest buildings in the world.

INTRODUCTION

LET'S EXPLORE SKYSCRAPERS

Have you ever traveled to a big city and seen its impressive skyline? Have you ever taken an elevator up, up, up to the top of a building that towers above the rest? Then you know how inspiring skyscrapers can be!

Skyscrapers are very tall buildings. They are so tall they seem to scrape at the sky. They are normally found in medium-sized to large cities around the world. Skyscrapers are used for offices, apartments, libraries, stores, restaurants, and much more.

WORDS TO KNOW

skyline: an outline of land and buildings against the sky.

skyscraper: an extremely tall building.

1

technology: the tools, methods, and systems used to solve a problem or do work.

engineer: a person who uses science, math, and creativity to design and build things such as roads, bridges, and buildings.

architect: a person who designs buildings.

engineering: the work an engineer does, using science and math to design and build things.

structure: something that is built, such as a building, bridge, tunnel, tower, or dam.

WORDS ᴛᴏ KNOW

Our definition of what a skyscraper is has changed during the past 100 years. This has happened as buildings have been built higher than ever before. Technology has helped engineers and architects construct taller and taller buildings.

During the nineteenth century, a skyscraper was any building that was 10 stories high or taller. But we wouldn't consider that to be a skyscraper today. Because of modern engineering, a skyscraper today typically reaches at least 40 to 50 stories tall, or around 550 feet in the air. That's about the size of 55 elephants stacked on top of one another!

EARLY SKYSCRAPERS

While the term *skyscraper* was first used in the year 1880, humankind has always enjoyed building tall structures.

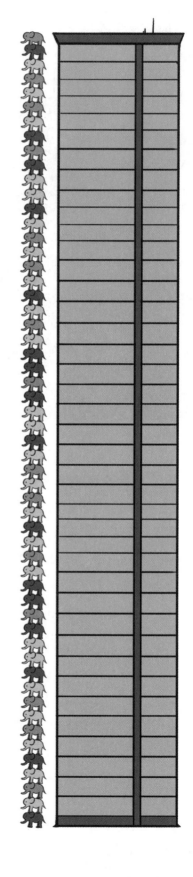

2

Even in the ancient world, architects often sought to build higher and higher into the sky. They thought it showed their dominance over nature and would impress others with their engineering know-how! And it was impressive.

HOW COME THE GIANT APE CLIMBED UP THE SIDE OF THE SKYSCRAPER?

HA HA HA

The elevator was broken!

dominance: power and influence over others.

coordination: the organization of different parts working together.

stable: firmly established and not likely to change or move.

physics: the science of how matter and energy work together. Matter is what an object is made of. Energy is the ability to perform work.

engineering design: the process engineers use to identify problems and come up with solutions.

predecessor: people, events, or things that came before.

WORDS ⏃ KNOW

It requires a lot of work, knowledge, and coordination to build a tall building that is stable. Tall buildings are built with many minds that know and use mathematics, the laws of physics, and engineering design methods.

Of course, we wouldn't call these ancient structures skyscrapers today. But they were the predecessors to the modern skyscrapers we see in cities today. Experiments done by early builders taught future architects and engineers how to build taller and stronger structures.

The town of Shibam in Yemen has been in existence for nearly 2,000 years. It has been called the "Manhattan of the Desert" and the "Ancient City of Skyscrapers." This is because Shibam's residents live in clay buildings that stand from 5 to 10 stories high. Evidence of construction on these ancient buildings has been dated to approximately 300 BCE, although most of the buildings were likely built after 1532 CE. They survive today as proof of the power of ancient engineering!

THE ANCIENT TOWN OF SHIBAM

But these were not the tallest buildings of the ancient world. That honor belongs to the Great Pyramid of Giza, which was built in ancient Egypt around 2500 BCE. This ancient pyramid stands nearly 480 feet tall.

While the pyramid is not exactly a skyscraper, its builders used many important architectural innovations. Some of these continue to boggle the minds of modern engineers today!

innovation: a new creation or a unique solution to a problem.

surpass: to be greater than something that came before.

WORDS TO KNOW

In fact, it is said that it took us thousands more years to be able to develop the technology to surpass this structure in height. The Lincoln Cathedral in England, built in the fourteenth century, was the first structure built that was taller than the Great Pyramid.

DID YOU KNOW?

The Great Pyramid once had a swivel door as an entrance. It was easy to push from the inside, but very hard to find from the outside, because it blended right in!

GOING UP

Of course, despite these early attempts at building tall structures, real skyscrapers began to be built only about 150 years ago. This was for two reasons.

First, to build a modern skyscraper, the frame of the building needs to be very strong. In engineering, the frame of a building is made of columns and beams. The columns are vertical and the beams are horizontal.

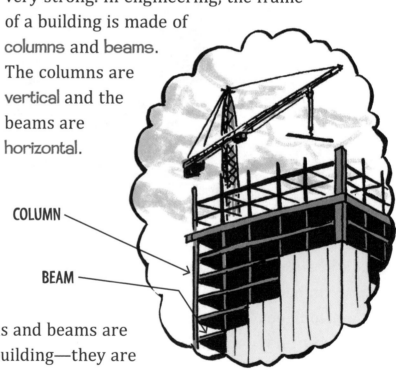

COLUMN

BEAM

Together, the columns and beams are like the skeleton of a building—they are what holds up the entire structure. But, during the early nineteenth century, humans did not yet have the technology to use very strong metal to build above about five stories. This would only come with the Industrial Revolution and the development of steel.

Also, to build higher structures, engineers needed to figure out how to get people all the way to the top of these buildings. How many stairs do you want to climb each time you go to your office or your apartment? Without a way to transport people to the top stories, the skyscrapers wouldn't be very useful.

Some ancient structures, such as the pyramids, were used as tombs for kings. People did not actually spend much time in them. Modern skyscrapers are different—they need to be accessible to be used as homes and offices.

The invention of the elevator in 1852 meant people could easily travel higher in taller buildings. Steel and elevators, two new technologies developed by engineers, made it possible to build taller and taller buildings.

GOOD ENGINEERING PRACTICES

Engineers and scientists keep their ideas organized in notebooks. Engineers use the engineering design process to keep track of their inventions, and scientists use the scientific method to keep track of experiments.

As you read through this book and do the activities, record your observations, data, and designs in an engineering design worksheet or a scientific method worksheet. When doing an activity, remember that there is no right answer or right way to approach a project. Be creative and have fun!

Engineering Design Worksheet
Problem: What problem are we trying to solve?
Research: Has anything been invented to help solve the problem? What can we learn?
Question: Are there any special requirements for the device? What is it supposed to do?
Brainstorm: Draw lots of designs for your device and list the materials you are using!
Prototype: Build the design you drew during brainstorming. This is your **prototype**.
Results: Test your prototype and record your observations.
Evaluate: Analyze your test results. Do you need to make adjustments? Do you need to try a different prototype?

Scientific Method Worksheet
Question: What problem are we trying to solve?
Research: What information is already known?
Hypothesis/Prediction: What do I think the answer will be?
Equipment: What supplies do I need?
Method: What steps will I follow?
Results: What happened and why?

This book is about skyscrapers and how they are made possible by teams of engineers and architects. It is also about the laws of nature. Physics determines whether a skyscraper will stand for hundreds—if not thousands—of years, or if it will never get off the ground.

> **earthquake:** a sudden movement in the outer layer of the earth.
>
> **gravity:** a force that pulls all objects toward the earth.
>
> **force:** a push or pull applied to an object.
>
> **WORDS TO KNOW**

In this book, you will learn how engineers and architects build skyscrapers so they are stable and safe. Tall buildings must be able to withstand wind, earthquakes, and the constant pull of the earth's gravity.

In order to understand how skyscrapers can stand so tall, you will build models and experiment with different materials and the forces that act on structures. You will examine how engineers follow the physical laws when building huge structures such as skyscrapers and how they experiment with the very limits of physics to build even higher. Sounds exciting, right? Let's dive in!

ESSENTIAL QUESTIONS

Each chapter of this book begins with an essential question to help guide your exploration of skyscrapers. Keep the question in your mind as you read the chapter. At the end of each chapter, use your engineering notebook to record your thoughts and answers.

?

INVESTIGATE!

Why are skyscrapers useful in big cities where there are lots of people?

PROJECT!

POWER PAPER!

SUPPLIES

* engineering notebook and pencil
* paper
* tape
* heavy books

Think about some words you might associate with paper, such as *thin* or *rip*, and then think of the words you might associate with a textbook, such as *heavy*. Do you think that sheets of paper could support the weight of one of your textbooks? Why or why not?

1 Start an engineering design worksheet in your engineering notebook. Your first step is to state the problem: How can you shape the paper in a way to make it strong enough to hold up a heavy book?

2 Consider different ways of folding, rolling, and taping your paper. Brainstorm and sketch your ideas. Choose a design to try. Make your paper and tape it to keep it in the shape you made. This is your prototype!

3 Test the strength of the shape by placing a heavy book on top of it. What happens? Do you need to change the way your paper is shaped? What can you do to the paper to make it stronger?

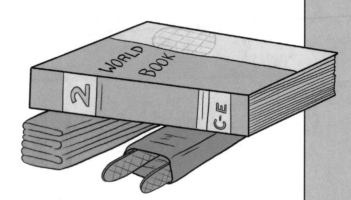

4 Change your design to make your paper stronger. Evaluate your new prototype. What shape is strongest? How much weight can you get your paper to hold?

EXPLORE MORE: What can you add to your paper structures to make them stronger? How does adding straws, popsicle sticks, or other material to your paper structures keep them from crumpling under the weight of the books?

THE GRANDFATHER OF SKYSCRAPERS

In England, you can still find the first building to be built with an iron frame, which was later developed into the technique of using steel frames to make taller buildings possible! In 1797, engineer Charles Bage (1751–1822) designed the Ditherington Flax Mill with an iron frame to help prevent fire. Flax dust was famous for going up in flames. The mill still stands. It is being renovated into offices and shops, while keeping the historic iron frame.

You can watch a short documentary about the building here.

KEYWORD PROMPTS

Ditherington Flax Mill video 🔍

CHAPTER ONE

WHY DO WE NEED SKYSCRAPERS?

We build skyscrapers today for many reasons. Some of these reasons have to do with our need to have lots of people in a small space. Some reasons have to do with the challenge of constructing buildings that are taller and taller!

In large cities, skyscrapers are a great way to fit lots of people into an area that takes up a small amount of ground. This becomes more important as cities grow larger and have more people living and working there.

 INVESTIGATE!

What might cities be like if there were no skyscrapers?

GIVE ME SPACE!

New York City is one of those cities known for its amazing skyscrapers. New York City is home to about 8.5 million people. But the city itself isn't very big. It sits on about 305 square miles of land. The island of Manhattan, which is part of the city, is slightly less than 23 square miles.

THE NEW YORK CITY SKYLINE

That's not much space for millions of people to live, work, and play. Plus, there are many more millions who travel to the city every day to work. And then there are the tourists who come to visit!

That's one reason why Manhattan is known for its skyscrapers. These buildings can house many more people in a smaller amount of space than regular buildings.

DID YOU KNOW?

September 3 is National Skyscraper Day. Celebrate this holiday by learning about a famous skyscraper architect or by visiting one of their creations!

ground area: the area of a building, which is calculated using its exterior measurements. Also called the footprint.

footprint: in architecture, the amount of ground covered by a building.

WORDS ⊕ KNOW

WHAT ANIMALS CAN JUMP HIGHER THAN A SKYSCRAPER?

HA HA HA HA

All of them! Skyscrapers can't jump.

Picture the average home in the United States. It is about 2,400 square feet. Let's say this house is made up of two stories and each story is about 1,200 square feet. That means that its ground area, or footprint, is 1,200 square feet. When you add the square footage of the two stories together, you get 2,400 square feet of space for everyone to sleep, eat, do homework, and relax!

However, a skyscraper might have 50 stories. If that skyscraper has the same ground area of 1,200 square feet and all of its stories are equally as large, then it doesn't just have a total area of 2,400 square feet like the house. Instead, it has 60,000 square feet! If a family of four can fit comfortably into 2,400 square feet, then 25 families could comfortably fit into the skyscraper—which has the same footprint as the house!

50 STORIES
60,000 SQUARE FEET
25 FAMILIES

2 STORIES
2,400 SQUARE FEET
1 FAMILY

CHALLENGE ACCEPTED

The need for space isn't the only reason we build skyscrapers. These buildings are incredible engineering feats that people are proud of designing and building. The urge to build bigger and better skyscrapers drives engineers and architects to find new, innovative ways of constructing these towers.

Engineers and architects have to find ways to defy gravity. Gravity is the force that pulls every person or thing to the ground. It is the reason why our feet stay firmly planted on the street rather than floating in the air. It is also the reason objects fall when we drop them.

feat: a product of skill or endurance.

defy: to challenge or resist.

counteract: to use an opposite force or action to work against something.

WORDS ⊕ KNOW

DID YOU KNOW?

Skyscrapers are built so they sway a bit in the wind. The Burj Khalifa in Dubai—with 163 stories above ground—can sway about 6.5 feet in each direction!

GRAVITY MYSTERIES

While we know many things about gravity, this force also remains a mystery to scientists. In particular, scientists don't understand why gravity appears to be so weak. For example, jump a couple of inches off the ground. You can do this easily, right? Scientists are still trying to discover why we can use the small force of our muscles to counteract the large gravitational force of the earth!

When engineers and architects build skyscrapers, they have to find a way to work against the downward pull of gravity as they construct upward. This can be done only if there is a strong support on the bottom of the tower. This support has to hold up all of the weight above it.

You have experienced this kind of weight if you've carried someone on your back. Imagine having to carry two people! You would need to be very strong and stable to be able to hold up that weight. It is the force of gravity that creates this weight.

Many engineers are fascinated by the challenge of building taller and taller buildings. They invent new and beautiful ways of supporting weight. Skyscrapers are some of the most impressive structures on Earth! Building skyscrapers is a way to test the limits of physical laws.

In the next chapter, we'll look at some of the forces of nature engineers need to consider when they build a skyscraper so that it stays standing, even during earthquakes!

 CONSIDER AND DISCUSS

It's time to consider and discuss: What might cities be like if there were no skyscrapers?

PROJECT!

SQUARE STABILITY

Which shape do you think is strongest, a triangle or a square? Why do you think so? Let's do an experiment and find out!

1 Start an engineering design or scientific method worksheet. What is your question or hypothesis? Write it down in your engineering notebook.

2 Connect straws to build shapes. To do this, insert the wider end of a paperclip in one straw. Next, hook a second paperclip to the first paperclip and pass the wider end of that paperclip into the second straw. You can build a square, a diamond, a rectangle, and a triangle.

3 Experiment with your shapes. Place your shapes upright on a table and press down on the top of each. What does the shape do? Does it bend or twist? How much force can you put on a shape before it collapses?

4 Which shape is the most stable? Was your hypothesis correct? Experiment with the least stable shape. Using no more than four paperclips and two straws, add to the shape to make it stronger. What did you do?

TRY THIS! Use the strongest shapes to build a tower. How much weight can your tower hold? Try placing paper or light books on top of the tower to test it. You can even weigh these objects afterward to see exactly how many ounces your structure can hold!

SKYSCRAPER SKELETONS

Challenge yourself to see how high you can build a structure using toothpicks and gumdrops as your building materials! You can also compete against your friends. Who can build the tallest skyscraper? At the end you can take your structures down and enjoy the gumdrops!

1 Start an engineering design worksheet. Brainstorm some ideas for building and sketch them in your notebook. Start by connecting your gumdrops and toothpicks to build a rectangle.

2 Test its stability by pressing down on the top of your structure. Does your structure seem stable? If not, how could you make it stronger?

3 As you build upward, experiment with different shapes, including squares, rectangles, and triangles. Which shape will allow you to build the strongest and tallest tower?

4 Build up, up, and up! Which tower is the highest? Why do you think that tower is higher than the other towers? Think about the shapes you have experimented with and the size of the base of your structure.

THINK MORE: Try to build a skyscraper out of toothpicks and gumdrops that has a wider top than base. Is there any way you can get this structure to stand without toppling over? If not, why?

PROJECT!

THE UNBREAKABLE EGG!

SUPPLIES

* 4 eggs
* books
* engineering notebook and pencil

We might think eggshells are very fragile, but in fact, they are very strong. Why? Because of the shape of the shell. In fact, this shape has been used in many buildings and skyscrapers since ancient times!

1 Notice the shape of your eggs. One end is pointier and the other end is rounder. Tap an egg on a hard surface to break it in half around the center, halfway between the pointy end and the round end. Ask an adult if you need help.

2 You can pour the egg into a bowl to make scrambled eggs later. Then discard the pointier half of the shell and keep the wider half. Rinse the inside of the shell.

3 Repeat this step with the other three eggs. Make sure your pieces are about the same size and height.

4 Place the four eggshells on a table in the shape of a rectangle with the broken ends down. Slowly place a book on top. Place another book to make a stack. How many books can you place on top of the eggshells before they break?

EXPLORE MORE: Why do you think eggs are so strong? Think about the curved shape of the egg and how this might distribute weight. How do engineers and architects use this shape to build strong structures?

WORDS to KNOW

fragile: easily broken.

19

PROJECT!

UP, UP, AND AWAY!

Elevators revolutionized architecture and made skyscrapers become a reality. How do elevators work? In this project, you can create your own elevator using a weight, a cable, and a counterweight**.**

SUPPLIES

* sheet of plywood or heavy cardboard
* nails
* 6 spindles from a craft shop
* scissors
* small cardboard box
* string
* small weight, such as a bolt or screw

1 Attach the spindles to the wooden board or cardboard, using nails so the spindles will be able to spin.

2 Make two holes in the top and bottom of the small cardboard box. Thread a short string through the top two holes and knot both ends to form a loop. Do the same thing for the bottom two holes.

3 Tie a long string to your bottom loop and pass it from the box under the bottom left spindles and up to the two top left spindles. Loop the string at least twice over the spindle on the corner. Tie this string to the string coming out of the top of the box.

4 Attach another string to the top of the box, bring it up and over the top right spindles, and attach it to your counterweight. Let your counterweight hang loosely from the right-most spindle.

5 Turn the top left spool. The elevator car should move up and down depending on the direction of your rotation of the spool.

WORDS TO KNOW

counterweight: a weight that balances another weight.

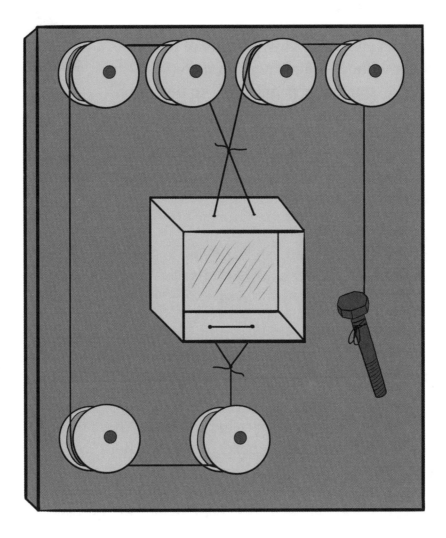

EXPLORE MORE: Counterweights provide balance in a mechanical system by adding an opposite force against the force exerted by the weight (such as the elevator in this experiment). What other mechanical systems use counterweights that you know of?

PROJECT!

NEWSPAPER TOWER

SUPPLIES

* engineering notebook and pencil
* 2 sheets of newspaper
* ruler

How tall can you build a tower made of newspaper without using any other materials— such as glue, staples, or paperclips—to hold it up?

1 Start an engineering design worksheet. What is your question and hypothesis. Use your ruler to make an educated guess and record your answer in your engineering notebook.

2 Build your tower. Keep experimenting to see how you can fold the paper to make your tower as tall as possible.

3 Evaluate your hypothesis. Was your tower as tall as you thought it would be? Was it shorter than you imagined? Why? What problems did you encounter when constructing the tower?

EXPLORE MORE: What would you do if you could use several inches of tape with the newspaper to build your tower. But you can't use the tape to secure your tower to the floor!

TRY IT! How much taller can you build the tower with this additional material?

Can you build a chair out of newspaper and tape that can hold your full weight? Many students have had fun experimenting with this project! **Learn more at this website.**

KEYWORD PROMPTS

PBS newspaper chair

CHAPTER TWO

ENGINEERING AND DESIGN

What happens when you drop something? Which way does it fall? You'd be pretty surprised if you dropped an apple and it floated up in the air instead of falling down to the ground! Why?

Everything in our world follows the laws of physics. These laws tell us how **energy** and **matter** will behave and interact with each other. We know about these physical laws from doing experiments and observing. These laws say that certain forces make things behave in certain ways.

> ## WORDS ☜ KNOW
>
> **energy:** the ability or power to do things, to work.
>
> **matter:** anything that has weight and takes up space.

23

INVESTIGATE!

What forces do engineers think about when designing a skyscraper?

compression: a pushing force that squeezes or presses material inward.

tension: a pulling force that pulls or stretches an object.

torsion: a twisting force.

shear: a sliding force that slips parts of a material in opposite directions.

mass: the amount of material that an object contains.

WORDS TO KNOW

When engineers design a skyscraper, they have to consider forces so the building will stay standing in different conditions. These forces include gravity, compression, tension, torsion, and shear.

GREAT GRAVITY

We all know that falling up is impossible in our world! That's because of gravity. Gravity is the force that pulls objects with mass toward Earth. Gravity is why an apple falls from a tree to the ground, why water runs downhill, and why the slides at the playground are so fun.

The more mass an object has, the more the force of gravity affects it. This is why it is extremely challenging to build very tall buildings, such as skyscrapers.

As skyscrapers get taller, they become heavier. This means the force of gravity becomes stronger. Engineers plan for the force of gravity by distributing weight along load-bearing walls. This makes sure that no one part of the building is holding up too much weight. Load-bearing walls hold up most of the weight of the building.

DID YOU KNOW?

Some forces that engineers need to consider when designing a building are specific to that particular building, while other forces are around us all the time. For example, gravity and friction are two forces that are at work all around us, all the time.

SHEARING FORCE

Shearing force is another force that can affect skyscrapers. This sliding force happens when different parts of the skyscraper are pushed and pulled in different directions.

Shearing force can be caused by earthquakes. A skyscraper must be able to withstand this force. Otherwise, it will crumble to the ground when the foundation it rests upon vibrates.

buckle: to collapse in the middle.

WORDS TO KNOW

COMPRESSION

Compression is a force that squeezes the materials of an object together. Think about what happens when you push down on a Slinky—the springs move until they are pushed together tightly. That's the force of compression.

In a building, compression occurs when the weight of a structure is too heavy for the materials that support it. If the force of compression is too strong, materials can buckle or snap. Either one of these results spells bad news for a structure!

TENSION

Tension and compression often work together. Think of a flagpole blowing in the wind. One side is stretched while the other side is crunched together. The side that stretches is experiencing tension. Tension pulls materials apart. This can happen with skyscrapers blowing in the wind.

What happens when you place a heavy object on a marshmallow? While parts of the marshmallow will be compressed, other parts will begin to experience tension and will spread apart. The base of the marshmallow will spread apart because of the weight above it.

The same thing can occur with skyscrapers. If the foundation cannot hold the weight above it, materials on the bottom tend to spread apart—and then the whole structure above it can collapse!

TORSION

Torsion is another word for "twisting." For example, if you hold a plastic ruler in your hands and twist both ends of it in opposite directions, what happens? Cracks will begin to form on the ruler as parts of it are pulled away from other parts. If this happens in a weight-bearing structure, such as a skyscraper, these cracks will become larger and larger until the structure is at risk of collapse.

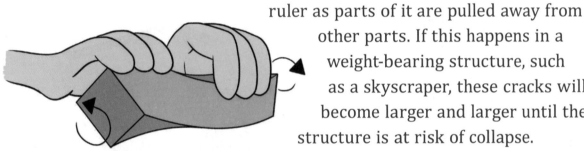

HOT AND COLD

Skyscrapers need to withstand changes in temperature. In some areas, such as Southern California, the temperature is same most of the time. In other areas, such as New York City, temperatures can change nearly 100 degrees Fahrenheit (38 degrees Celsius) depending on the time of year.

DID YOU KNOW?

A skyscraper built in the United Arab Emirates, where it's very hot and dry, might need to use different materials and techniques than a skyscraper built in Canada, where it's very cold!

lateral force: a force applied to the sides of an object.

WORDS TO KNOW

Hot temperatures can cause materials to expand, or get bigger, while cold temperatures cause materials to contract, or get smaller. Have you ever seen cracks in the road after a cold winter? These cracks are caused from the cold making the road material shrink.

The same thing can happen to a skyscraper! Engineers think carefully about their materials to prevent this kind of damage.

WINDY FORCE

Have you ever been on the top story of a skyscraper? What about high in a tree? You might notice the wind!

As you go higher and higher, there is greater wind force. Wind can cause a skyscraper to sway from side to side. This is called a lateral force.

DID YOU KNOW?

At a certain height above the earth, the wind dies down. This is why airplanes fly above wind patterns—at about 33,000 feet in the air!

Engineers need to do two things to counteract lateral force. They need to make the skyscraper **flexible** so that the building doesn't simply snap when it sways in the wind. The skyscraper also needs to have a strong support to hold it up against the wind.

SOIL SCIENCE

Engineers don't just analyze the building materials, they must also analyze the ground on which their structure will be built. Special engineers called geotechnical engineers investigate the soil where construction is planned. Is it rocky? Is it strong enough to hold up a large structure?

WHY DID THE GARDENER PLANT HIS MONEY?

HA HA HA

He wanted the soil to be rich.

PS How long does it take to build a skyscraper? In 2015, a company in China built a 57-story skyscraper in 19 days. **You can watch a video of the entire project at this website.**

KEYWORD PROMPTS

Guardian China skyscraper

WORDS TO KNOW

borehole: a deep and narrow hole drilled into the ground to study the soil or to locate water.

soil core: a sample of soil to examine and test, shaped like the tube that was used to remove it.

efficient: wasting as little as possible.

These engineers drill **boreholes** in the ground and remove soil samples in long, clear tubes called **soil cores**. Then, they analyze the soil samples for quality, water content, pollution, or anything else that may affect the structure that will be built on top!

MEET THE ENGINEERS

Engineers use their knowledge of science and math to develop creative solutions to problems. To build a skyscraper, they need to understand what building materials should be used, how much weight these materials can support, and what design will be the strongest.

Engineers use the scientific method to create solutions to everyday problems. They start with a problem and brainstorm different ways to solve that problem. They choose several solutions that could work and then experiment with these solutions.

For example, an engineer might need to think of an **efficient** way to pump water up to the top of a tall skyscraper. Engineers do lots of creative thinking!

SKETCHING WITH SKETCHUP

Architects and engineers use very advanced computer **modeling** programs that can figure out how materials should be put together and what forces they can withstand. Many engineering computer programs are very expensive and are available only to professional engineers and architects. However, one program that you can use for free is SketchUp. It allows you to create **three-dimensional (3-D)** models.

You can find out more about SketchUp and download it at this website.

KEYWORD PROMPTS

SketchUp 🔍

Civil engineers design and build roads, bridges, canals, dams, and buildings, including skyscrapers. Without civil engineers, no skyscraper would ever get off the ground.

Almost all major cities have soaring skyscrapers! In the next chapter, we'll learn about the different types of skyscrapers and how engineers decide which kind to build.

WORDS ⊙ KNOW

model: a miniature, three-dimensional representation of something to be constructed.

three-dimensional (3-D): an image that has length, width, and height, and is raised off the flat page.

civil engineer: an engineer who designs structures such as buildings, roads, bridges, and tunnels.

? **CONSIDER AND DISCUSS**

It's time to consider and discuss: What forces do engineers think about when designing a skyscraper?

PROJECT!

SHAKE AWAY!

Skyscrapers need to be able to withstand movement, whether it's from wind or an earthquake! In this experiment, you'll build your own shake table **and then test the strength of your skyscrapers.**

1 Place the two pieces of cardboard on top of one another. Connect them by stretching rubber bands around each end, about 1 inch from each end.

2 Place a rubber ball between the layers of cardboard in each corner, about 2 inches in from each end. This is your shake table.

3 Attach the Lego plate to the top of the shake table by placing it underneath the top rubber band.

4 Build different Lego towers of varying heights and shapes. Keep their footprints the same. Then, attach one Lego tower at a time to the center of the Lego plate on the shake table.

5 Twist the top piece of cardboard away from the bottom piece of cardboard while keeping the top section flat. Measure how far you pulled the top layer away from the bottom layer and record this in your journal. This is called displacement.

WORDS ⏺ KNOW

shake table: a platform that simulates the shaking caused by an earthquake.

displacement: when something is moved by an object taking its place.

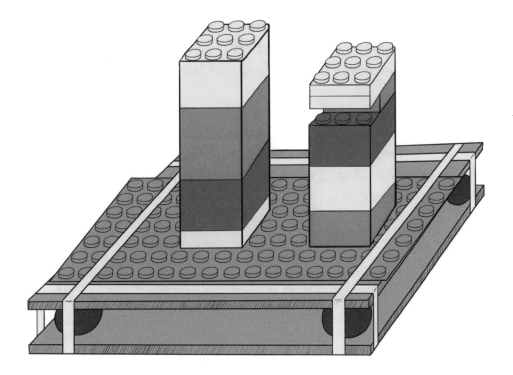

6 Record your observations of your towers at different displacements. Which tower remains standing at the greatest displacement? The tallest tower or the shortest tower? Record your results in your engineering notebook.

THINK ABOUT IT: How might architects and engineers use experiments with shake tables to design buildings that can withstand earthquakes? What might they learn from such experiments that can change how they engineer buildings?

TUG, TWIST, AND PULL

In this experiment, you can use common household materials to build a tower and test how it withstands forces such as tension, compression, and torsion.

SUPPLIES

* ❋ engineering notebook and pencil
* ❋ 3 popsicle sticks
* ❋ 3 pipe cleaners
* ❋ 3 lumps of clay
* ❋ 3 rubber bands
* ❋ 3 paper-towel tubes
* ❋ 3 pieces of aluminum foil

1 Start an engineering design worksheet. Which materials will be strongest against tension? Against compression? Against torsion? Which material will be the strongest overall? The weakest overall?

2 Make a table for your results based on the following rating scale.

1	Very weak! It crumples or breaks with hardly any force.
2	Only fair! It can't withstand much force.
3	Pretty good! It takes a lot of force to break it.
4	Super strong! We can't break it.

3 Test how each material reacts to tension. To test tension, pull both ends of the material outward. Record your observations and rating.

4 Test how each material reacts to compression. To test compression, push the material together at both ends. Record your observations and your rating.

PROJECT!

5 Test how each material reacts to torsion. To test torsion, twist the two ends of the material in different directions. Record your observations and rating.

6 How did your results compare to your hypothesis? Which material was the strongest? The weakest? Why?

THINK ABOUT IT: Do you think some materials might be stronger against some forces, such as torsion, but weaker against other forces, such as compression or tension? How might engineers solve such a problem?

DID YOU KNOW?

Graphene is the world's strongest building material! Amazingly, it is made up of only a single layer of carbon atoms. Skyscrapers of the future might make use of this rediscovered material!

Material	Tension	Compression	Torsion	Total
popsicle sticks				
pipe cleaners				

PROJECT!

CRAZY COLUMNS

Using toilet paper tubes filled up with different materials, you can experiment with how these different materials can bear weight without collapsing. Which material will be the strongest?

SUPPLIES

* ✳ 4 toilet paper tubes
* ✳ masking tape
* ✳ tissues
* ✳ popcorn kernels
* ✳ timer
* ✳ sand
* ✳ engineering notebook and pencil

1 Start an engineering design or scientific method worksheet. Then prepare the tubes, using masking tape to cover the bottom of each tube so that anything you put inside won't fall out.

2 Leave one tube empty. Fill the next tube with bunched up tissues, the next with popcorn kernels, and the final tube with sand.

3 Close the top of each tube with masking tape so that you can shake the tube and nothing will come out.

4 Which tube do you think will be the strongest? Which will be the weakest? Why? Write your ideas down in your notebook.

5 Place the empty tube on the floor near a railing or wall. Holding onto the railing or wall, step onto the tube. How long does it take to collapse? Write your observations down in a chart.

6 Do the same thing for the other remaining tubes. Each time, estimate first how long it will take for each tube to collapse. Write down your observations of what happens.

7 Which was the weakest column? Which was the strongest column? Why? Was your hypothesis correct?

TRY THIS! See if you can find other simple materials to put in toilet paper tubes and continue your experiment. You can use gravel, dirt, woodchips, or even mud (although this might be a bit messy!).

Material	Hypothesis	Actual Time

ANCIENT WORLD WONDER

The Lighthouse of Alexandria is one of the Seven Wonders of the Ancient World and was the tallest man-made structure in antiquity. Built around 280 BCE in Alexandria, Greece, it reportedly stood at around 328 feet tall. Unfortunately, the lighthouse was later damaged during several earthquakes, and was completely destroyed in the fifteenth century.

(PS) View a 1909 drawing of the Lighthouse of Alexandria by German archaeologist Hermann Thiersch. An archaeologist studies ancient people through the objects they left behind.

KEYWORD PROMPTS

Lighthouse Thiersch 🔍

PROJECT!

YOU GLUED IT

Different materials work together in different ways. For example, one type of glue might work better on plastic while another type might work better with fabric or wood. Engineers need to know how physical forces might act on their structures, but must also understand how the materials they use work together.

> **Caution:** Use the glue and the electric drill only with the supervision of an adult.

1 Start an engineering design or scientific method worksheet. Which glue do you think will be the strongest when used with plywood? Which will be the weakest? Why?

2 Have an adult help you drill two holes through the center of the small piece of plywood, about 2 inches apart.

3 Pass two ends of a wire up through the holes and tie at the top of the board. There should be enough slack in the wire hanging down for you to hang the S-hook on it.

4 Glue the smaller sheet of plywood to the larger sheet using one of your glues. Check the glue's instructions and wait for the recommended time so it will dry properly.

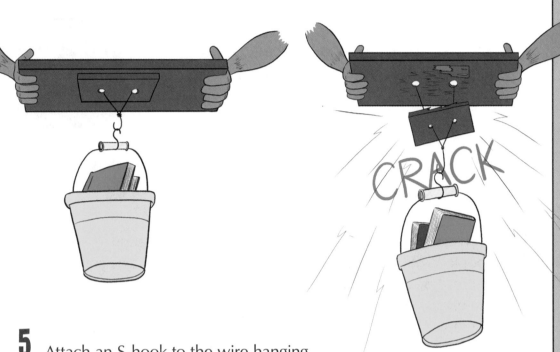

CRACK

5 Attach an S-hook to the wire hanging down from the plywood and hang a bucket from it. Add one book at a time to the bucket. Keep filling the bucket until the glue no longer holds and the boards fall apart. How many books were in the bucket when it broke?

6 Repeat steps 2–5 using each kind of glue that you are experimenting with. Which glue held the most amount of weight? Which glue held the least amount of weight? Why do you think this is? Record your answer in your engineering notebook.

TRY THIS! Experiment with different kinds of wood to see if the type of wood makes a difference. You can also try clamping the wood together while the glue is drying to see if this makes a difference.

SOIL SAMPLES

In this project, you can use clear straws as soil cores to investigate the soil in your backyard. Can you find soil that would be good for building on?

1 Pick two spots in your backyard that you think might have different kinds of soil. Use the shovel to loosen the soil in these spots.

2 Start a scientific method worksheet in your engineering design notebook. Write down your hypothesis. Do you think one soil sample will be better than another? Why or why not? Write down the characteristics of soil that would best support a large structure such as a skyscraper.

3 Take a soil core in one of your chosen spots by pressing a clear plastic straw into the ground. If it is too hard to force down, twist it in as far as it will go. Label the straw to identify the spot where you took the soil. Repeat at the second spot you picked. Label this straw.

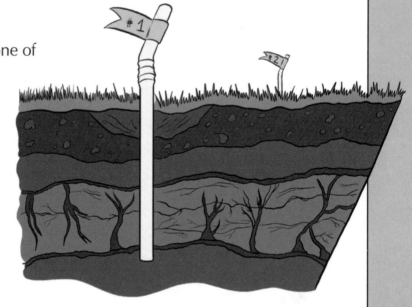

4 Use scissors to gently cut open one straw while keeping the core sample intact. Place the core sample on labeled white paper to identify the sample. It is okay if the core sample breaks apart. Write down your observations about the core sample in your notebook. Repeat for the second core sample.

5 Using the observations you've written about each core sample in your notebook, decide whether one sample would better support the weight of a structure than the other sample. Why or why not? Does your conclusion match your hypothesis? Why or why not?

THINK ABOUT IT: If the soil in a certain area cannot support a foundation on top of it, what other options might engineers explore to strengthen the base of their building?

CORE SAMPLES FROM THE DEMOCRATIC REPUBLIC OF THE CONGO
(CREDIT: U.S. DEPARTMENT OF AGRICULTURE)

COMPRESSION AND TENSION TUBES

SUPPLIES

* 6 toilet paper tubes
* toilet paper
* wax paper
* engineering notebook and pencil

Throughout history, architects and engineers have used different shapes to bear weight in large structures. For example, the ancient Egyptians built large structures in the shape of (you guessed it!) pyramids. In this experiment, you can use different materials in the shape of a pyramid to experiment with how they withstand the forces of compression and tension.

1 Lay the toilet paper tubes horizontally to build a pyramid. Does the structure stay in place or does it fall apart? Why?

2 Try wrapping each tube in a layer of toilet paper to get the tubes to stay in a pyramid shape. Does this help the pyramid to stay up or not? Why?

3 Try placing a layer of toilet paper between each layer of the pyramid as you build up. Does this help the pyramid to stay up or not? Why? Why might one way of using toilet paper to hold up the pyramid work while the other does not?

4 Try steps 2 and 3 using wax paper instead of toilet paper. How do the results compare to the toilet paper? Write down your observations in your notebook.

THINK ABOUT IT: In addition to pyramids, what other shape was commonly used by ancient architects to strengthen their buildings?

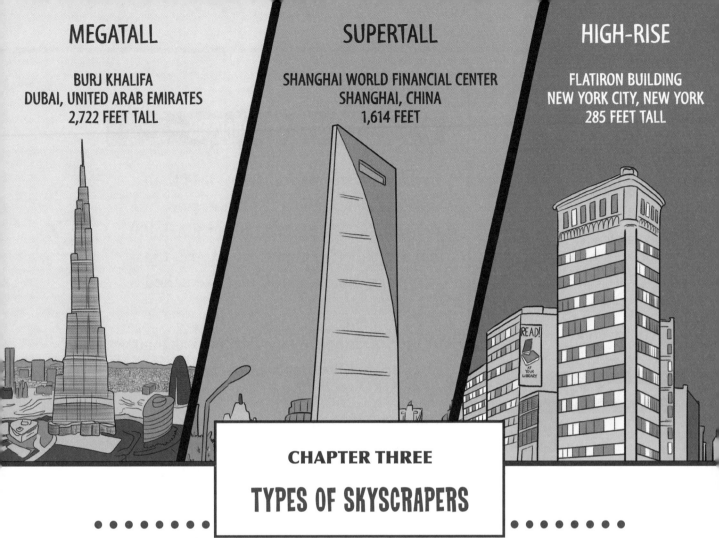

MEGATALL

BURJ KHALIFA
DUBAI, UNITED ARAB EMIRATES
2,722 FEET TALL

SUPERTALL

SHANGHAI WORLD FINANCIAL CENTER
SHANGHAI, CHINA
1,614 FEET

HIGH-RISE

FLATIRON BUILDING
NEW YORK CITY, NEW YORK
285 FEET TALL

CHAPTER THREE

TYPES OF SKYSCRAPERS

In the nineteenth century, a skyscraper was a building that reached about 10 stories high. By today's standards, that's pretty short! During the past 100 years, engineers have been able to build taller and stronger skyscrapers. Now, a building is only considered a skyscraper if it reaches past 40 or 50 stories.

Today, there are many different kinds of skyscrapers. There are also different engineering techniques to achieve the soaring heights of today's skyscrapers.

? INVESTIGATE!

How are we able to build taller and taller skyscrapers?

43

WORDS TO KNOW

high-rise: a building with many stories and with elevators, typically used for housing or offices.

supertall: a skyscraper that is more than 984 feet tall.

megatall: a skyscraper that is more than 1,969 feet tall.

demolish: to tear down.

riveted: connected with metal bolts called rivets.

TYPES OF SKYSCRAPERS

Smaller skyscrapers that are less than 984 feet are often called high-rises. Skyscrapers that reach more than 1,000 feet are called supertall, and those that stretch to almost 2,000 feet are called megatall.

The first modern skyscraper was a large steel box with different boxes contained inside of it. The use of steel, a strong metal, allowed engineers to construct taller buildings. The first skyscraper in the world to use steel was the Home Insurance Building, a 10-story building constructed in Chicago, Illinois, in 1885. This building was demolished in 1931.

CAST IRON VS. STEEL

Before steel, cast iron was typically used in tall buildings. But cast iron has many problems. First, cast iron is much heavier than steel, which means buildings could not be as tall. Second, cast iron is less flexible than steel, which means that it can't be formed into different shapes. Steel, unlike cast iron, can also be riveted, which means it can be connected using large metal bolts. Without the introduction of steel in the late nineteenth century, skyscrapers as we know them today wouldn't exist. Today, steel has completely replaced iron as the building material of choice for tall structures.

When the Home Insurance Building was first built, Chicago officials were nervous about whether or not steel could bear the weight of the building. In fact, they stopped construction for some time so that they could investigate how safe the structure really was. In this steel-frame design, vertical columns and horizontal I-beams made of steel held up the structure. Officials were surprised to find that this design could hold up its own weight.

The steel-frame design was also about one-third lighter than stone. This allowed skyscrapers to stretch much higher, because the structure wasn't as heavy.

In skyscraper engineering, the structure must hold up

two types of weight, called loads. The dead load is the weight of the structure itself. This is usually much more than the live load, which is the weight of all of the people and things inside the structure. Early skyscraper engineers realized that this meant the lower levels of the skyscraper needed more material and weight than the upper levels.

45

shear wall: a paneled wall that is used to distribute weight in heavy buildings.

framed tube: a type of frame used in skyscrapers to distribute and decrease weight loads.

WORDS TO KNOW

One of the early inventions that helped make skyscrapers stronger was a shear wall. A shear wall stretches from the ground to the top of the building—the whole wall supports the loads. It supports lateral loads that are felt side to side, such as from the wind blowing. It also supports vertical loads—the weight that comes from the top down to the ground.

However, shear walls are not enough to support the total weight of a large skyscraper. Engineers had to invent new techniques. In early skyscrapers, engineers built a large steel box with smaller boxes inside. This worked for skyscrapers up to around 40 stories tall, but the technique wasn't efficient for taller structures. This way of building increased the load and forced more of the space in the building to be used for support instead of for offices or living spaces.

FRAMED TUBES

To help solve the weight problem, in 1963, an engineer named Fazlur Rahman Khan (1929–1982) came up with a technique called a framed tube. In this design, a hollow column is built into the ground, and the skyscraper is built around this core.

CORE

The good thing about the framed tube design was that fewer columns were needed inside the structure. It opened up more usable space in the skyscraper. Framed tube construction was first used in the DeWitt-Chestnut Apartment Building in Chicago. Later, the John Hancock Center and the World Trade Center towers were built using this kind of construction.

Builders can also use a bundled-tube frame when constructing a skyscraper. With bundled-tube frames, several interconnecting tubes are used to form the main structure. This lets architects change the look of the structures. They can group frames together to create more interesting buildings.

FAZLUR RAHMAN KHAN

Known as the grandfather of tubular skyscrapers, Khan made many important contributions to the field of structural engineering. Born in modern-day Bangladesh in 1929, he came to study in the United States. During the 1950s, Khan discovered that building skyscrapers around central tubes to distribute loads allowed engineers and architects to build taller buildings because the internal structure is lighter. Now, almost all skyscrapers that are built around the world use this system. Khan also pioneered **computer-aided design (CAD)** and designed the Sears Tower, now called the Willis Tower, located in Chicago. This was the tallest building in the world from 1973 until 1998. Our cities today would not be recognizable without Khan's many contributions.

x-bracing: diagonal support beams that intersect to provide more stability for a structure.

truss: a network of beams and bars that relies on triangles to support a load.

WORDS ⊙ KNOW

X-BRACING

Another structural engineering technique is x-bracing. This is a way of building skyscrapers that lets outside columns take some of the load by placing x-bracing and trusses at important points.

This technique is also known as the braced tube or the trussed tube. These elements transfer the weight of the building from the middle part of the structure to the sides of the structure. This means the building can carry more weight, plus it opens up the inside, because fewer interior columns are needed to support the weight of the whole building.

X-bracing was first used in the construction of the Singer Building in New York City in 1908. At the time, the Singer Building was the tallest building in the world. In 1968, it was torn down to make space for what would become One Liberty Plaza, another famous skyscraper in Lower Manhattan.

In 1969, x-bracing was famously used in the John Hancock Center, a 100-story skyscraper in Chicago. The x-bracing became part of the outside design of the building.

THE JOHN HANCOCK CENTER (CREDIT: ROMAN BOED)

WORDS ᴛᴏ KNOW

setback: a flat offset in a wall.

recession: a part of a structure or wall that goes in from the main part.

SETBACKS

Many of today's skyscrapers include an innovation called setbacks, also called step-backs. These are recessions in a wall that change the way weight is distributed in skyscrapers.

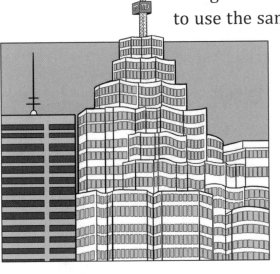

Imagine building a tower out of blocks. Is it easier to use the same size block going all the way up or is it easier to use a smaller and smaller size block the higher you get?

Ancient engineers discovered that they could make each level have a smaller footprint as they went higher. The building was then more balanced than if it was built straight up and down with no setbacks.

SCAMMED!

The Newby-McMahon Building in Wichita Falls, Texas, is known as the World's Littlest Skyscraper. According to local legend, the structural engineer J.D. McMahon proposed to build a high-rise in 1919. He collected the equivalent of nearly $3 million to begin building, although he had no intention of building a skyscraper. Instead, McMahon built a much smaller building at about 40 feet tall and pocketed the rest of the money! Today, the small, four-story Newby-McMahon Building is considered a Texas Historic Landmark.

ziggurat: a stepped tower with a temple on top.

Mesopotamia: a region of the Middle East that today is part of Iraq.

WORDS TO KNOW

CONSIDER AND DISCUSS

It's time to consider and discuss: How are we able to build taller and taller skyscrapers?

However, with the use of steel frames to build skyscrapers in the early twentieth century, setbacks were no longer needed. But people still use them because they allow natural light to reach the street and buildings below the skyscraper.

In the next chapter, we'll take a look at the long, complicated process of building a skyscraper. It begins with deciding on a design and continues through the entire building process!

DID YOU KNOW?

Setbacks have been used by engineers for thousands of years, and can be seen in some of the earliest and largest buildings in human civilization, including the **ziggurats** of ancient Mesopotamia.

ZIGGURATS AND TEMPLES IN ANCIENT MESOPOTAMIA

PROJECT!

TOOTHPICK TRUSS

SUPPLIES

* toothpicks
* gumdrops
* engineering notebook and pencil

Using toothpicks and gumdrops, you can experiment with trusses and how different kinds of trusses can bear weight.

1 Use toothpicks and gumdrops to create a rectangular structure as shown in the illustration.

2 Test your rectangular structure by pressing down on top of it and wiggling it. How much movement do you feel? Write down your observations in your engineering notebook.

3 How would you use additional materials to strengthen your structure? Start an engineering design worksheet. Are there shapes you can use other than squares?

4 After you strengthen your structure, press down on it and wiggle it again. Do you feel less movement than you felt before?

5 Could you use fewer materials to strengthen your structure? Why or why not? Keep experimenting to see how you can strengthen your structure with the fewest materials.

EXPLORE MORE: With an adult's permission, look online to get a better idea of what trusses look like. See if you can find the most ancient truss in existence today!

PROJECT!

WIND WHOOPS

The force exerted by wind is something that all architects and engineers must keep in mind when designing buildings. In this experiment, you can see how wind force might affect different structures. Use an engineering design worksheet to keep your ideas organized.

SUPPLIES

* ✳ several sheets of cardstock or thick paper
* ✳ tape
* ✳ table
* ✳ glue
* ✳ scissors
* ✳ toothpick
* ✳ ruler
* ✳ blow dryer
* ✳ engineering notebook and pencil

1 Glue or tape together four sheets of cardstock to make a rectangular skyscraper. Cut out a square to make a roof and tape that in place.

2 Cut several lengthwise strips from another piece of cardstock. Then, cut these strips into smaller tabs of about 3 inches each. Making sure one side of the skyscraper is up against a wall, tape these tabs onto the bottom of the skyscraper and then tape the tabs at the bottom of the skyscraper onto a table to secure it.

3 On the back of your skyscraper, tape a toothpick on the right-hand corner. It should stick up at least 1 inch from your skyscraper. On the wall behind your skyscraper, tape a ruler horizontally so that the toothpick points at the zero.

4 Use a blow dryer about 1 foot from your skyscraper. Put it on the lowest setting at first and observe how far the toothpick (and your skyscraper) moves. Record the measurement. Now do the same thing with the blow dryer at its highest setting. This will show you the **sway** of your building.

WORDS ᴛᴏ KNOW

sway: the distance that a building can move from side to side.

5 Take another sheet of cardstock and use scissors to cut strips lengthwise about 1 inch wide. Glue or tape the strips of cardstock to the skyscraper as shown, so that each side of the structure has an X-shaped support.

6 Use your blow dryer again at the lowest setting and then the highest setting and record your answers. How did adding the X-bracing change the sway on your skyscraper?

EXPLORE MORE: Build more skyscrapers in the same way and experiment with different patterns of trusses. Which design uses the least amount of material? Which looks the best? Can you design a system of trusses that works well, doesn't add too much weight, and also looks good?

TRUSS ME!

Trusses are a framework of beams that are designed to make a structure stronger than a single beam. They are designed to look like many crisscrossing triangles, because triangles are the strongest shapes that cannot bend or twist. Trusses are commonly used to strengthen bridges and skyscrapers. They also hold up the roofs of most buildings.

SUPPLIES

* tongue depressors
* tape
* scissors
* plastic cup
* string
* books
* quarters
* engineering notebook and pencil

1 Use the tongue depressors and tape to create a square and a triangle. Experiment with pulling the sides of each structure. Which seems stronger?

2 Build more square structures from the tongue depressors. Use tape to make them into a box-shaped larger structure.

DID YOU HEAR ABOUT THE ROOF'S RELATIONSHIP?

HA HA HA

It was built on truss.

3 Using scissors, make a small hole in both sides of the plastic cup. Pass a string through one side of the cup, then over the center of your box-shaped structure, and back through the other side of the plastic cup. Tie off the strings. The cup should now be hanging evenly from the center of your structure.

4 Make two piles of books. The piles should be the same height. Rest your structure evenly between the books.

5 Place one quarter inside the cup. Does the structure move or sway? Does it collapse? Write down your observations.

6 Keep adding more quarters until the structure can no longer hold up the weight. How many quarters were you able to place into the cup before the structure collapsed?

7 Make a truss structure by building and connecting triangle structures. Insert string through the cup and around the structure so that it hangs down from the center.

8 Repeat steps 5 and 6 to test your new structure. How many quarters can the truss structure hold before it collapses?

EXPLORE MORE: Which structure was able to hold up more weight? Why? Can you make your structure even stronger? How?

PROJECT!

EXPLORING COMPRESSION AND TENSION

SUPPLIES
* permanent marker
* sponge

Compression and tension are two complementary forces that can occur when an object is bent. You will do an experiment to see these two forces at work!

1 Using a permanent marker, draw **parallel** lines lengthwise across the front and back of the sponge. Now, bend the sponge into the shape of a U.

2 What happens to the lines on the sponge? Why do some lines seem to grow farther apart while some lines seem closer together? Which lines on the sponge show compression? Which lines on the sponge show tension?

THINK ABOUT IT: How might this sponge show what happens to building materials such as wood or steel? Which material (wood or steel) do you think would show the most compression or tension? Why?

DID YOU KNOW?

In 1981, a man named Dan Goodwin dressed up in a handmade Spiderman costume and climbed the Sears Tower using suction cups and hooks! Goodwin wanted to make people understand that rescue procedures for skyscrapers weren't good enough.

WORDS ⊕ KNOW

complementary: forces that work together.

parallel: anything that is always the same distance away from something else.

PROJECT!

TESTING MATERIALS

Engineers need to know if a material is ductile, **which means it can bend easily without breaking, or** brittle, **which means it will shatter or break instead of bending. In this activity, you'll test some materials!**

SUPPLIES

* soda can
* plastic bottle
* quarter
* cardboard
* engineering notebook and pencil

1 Start a scientific method worksheet. Take all four materials—soda can, bottle, quarter, and cardboard—and line them up on a table. Examine each one and write down your observations about the material. Which do you think will be the strongest? Why?

2 Try to categorize each material as ductile or brittle. Are there any that don't fit into either category? Why? Why might this be an advantage—or a disadvantage—for civil engineers?

3 Categorize the materials as weakest or strongest at bearing weight. Experiment by pressing down on these materials or attempting to bend them. For the strongest material, what might its drawbacks be? Why might it be a difficult material to work with? For the weakest material, what might be its advantages?

THINK MORE: Think about other materials that you might have in your house, such as sponges, wood, glass, or fabrics. Write down each material and hypothesize whether you think these materials are ductile or brittle. What happens when you press down on these materials and attempt to bend them?

WORDS TO KNOW

ductile: bendable without breaking.

brittle: easily broken, cracked, or snapped.

57

PROJECT!

HANGING IN THE BALANCE

SUPPLIES

* ✱ 6 books of the same or similar size
* ✱ several quarters
* ✱ table

In this experiment, books are stacked so that they hang off a table. The table represents the core of a skyscraper, which is the strongest part of the structure and needs to hold all the weight above it. The books represent a cantilever**, which supports the floors of the building. And the coins represent the weight of the floors that the cantilever must hold.**

1 Arrange a book so that 2 inches of it are hanging off the edge of the table. Put another book on top of the first book so that it hangs 1 to 2 inches off the first one. Then put another book on top of the second book and keep doing this until all six books are stacked. On top of the sixth book, stack the quarters.

2 Experiment with the way the books are arranged. Change them so that some stick out farther than others. How does this affect the way the structure is able to hold weight? Experiment to see when the structure fails—when the quarters or the books fall.

TRY THIS! With an adult's permission, do an online search for cantilevers and see how they are used. Do you think cantilevers can be used to make a building look nicer?

Watch fifth-graders design and build cantilevers! What types of material are they using? How does this add strength to their structures?

KEYWORD PROMPTS

fifth grade cantilevers 🔍

WORDS TO KNOW

cantilever: a long beam that is fixed to a building or structure at only one end.

CHAPTER FOUR

LET THE BUILDING BEGIN!

What does it take to build a skyscraper? Lots of time and lots of people! From making the plans to breaking ground, building the supports, and finishing the roof, building a skyscraper is a complicated project. It involves large teams of people working together.

How do all these people know what to do? Before any building begins, the leaders of the project, including the architects, engineers, and the construction team, talk about the scope of the project. They make a detailed plan about how the building process is going to work.

? INVESTIGATE!

Why does it take such strong teamwork to build a skyscraper?

project coordination: the organization of all steps required to complete a building project.

natural disaster: a natural event, such as a fire or flood, that causes great damage.

acoustical engineer: an engineer who works with sound and the way sound travels through spaces.

WORDS ⊕ KNOW

HOW DO CONSTRUCTION WORKERS PARTY?

HA HA HA

They raise the roof.

This is called project coordination. A project coordinator makes sure everyone working on the skyscraper knows their job. Here are some of the jobs it takes to build a skyscraper from the ground up.

DEVELOPMENT

After plans are drawn up, specialists test different parts of the plan to make sure the building will be safe and useful. During this step, 3-D computer models are often used. This allows engineers to make sure the building will be fine, even in earthquakes, major storms, and other natural disasters.

The team might conduct wind-tunnel tests to make sure a building can withstand heavy winds. Fire safety tests are another important step. Fire safety engineers can build scale models of skyscrapers and then subject them to very high temperatures to see what would happen to the building materials.

Geotechnical engineers examine the soil before deciding where to build and what materials to use for a foundation. Sometimes, acoustical engineers make sure sound doesn't travel too much between floors or down elevator shafts.

Mechanical engineers review elevator systems, as well as heating and cooling systems. Public health engineers work on the air quality and water systems in a building.

All of these specialists do a lot of work on the skyscraper before building begins!

ZONING

Once the plans are in place, they must be approved. Through zoning and permits, a city makes sure builders follow the rules when developing new construction. For example, it might be illegal to build a tower above a certain height in a certain area. During the permitting process, all plans are checked to make sure they follow the rules.

Sometimes, people in the neighborhood will review building plans and ask the local government to stop the structure from being built. They might be worried that a large building will prevent sunlight from reaching their own apartments. They might be concerned that a new skyscraper will mean far more

A WORKER CONSTRUCTING THE EMPIRE STATE BUILDING. (CREDIT: LEWIS HINE)

traffic in the neighborhood. These are the kinds of worries that are addressed during the permitting process.

Finally, when all of these steps are done, building can begin. Construction is a long process—it can take many years!

IT'S FOUNDATIONAL!

When building begins, it is important for the team to get the foundation right. It's what holds up the whole building!

Often, demolition is the first step so the space is clear and ready for building. Then, soil scientists test and re-test the soil to make sure it is suitable for building. If the ground needs to be higher or lower, truckloads of soil or gravel might be brought in or taken out.

DID YOU KNOW?

Washington, DC, has no skyscrapers! No building can be higher than 130 feet.

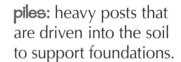

Then, workers begin laying the foundation. Two types of foundations that are often used are driven piles and caissons. Driven piles are made through a process called piling, which involves drilling a deep hole and filling it with concrete and rebar or steel bars. The concrete must dry, or cure, before it is built upon. This can take several weeks.

Caissons are watertight, hollow structures that engineers fill with concrete and then bury in the ground. They are often used to build the foundations of bridges or dams. Caissons are also good for skyscrapers that are being built on soil that is particularly muddy or soggy.

Once the groundwork is done, pile caps and steel beams are connected to the pilings. Some structures are lined with steel forms, which are then filled with more concrete and rebar. When the pilings and pile caps are completed, a concrete slab is poured and the building is ready to rise!

piles: heavy posts that are driven into the soil to support foundations.

caisson: a hollow, waterproof structure that can be filled with cement to form the basis of foundations.

concrete: a hard construction material made with cement, sand, and water.

rebar: steel bars that are put into concrete to make it stronger.

pile cap: a thick layer of concrete that rests on piles that were driven into the ground to form a stable foundation.

concrete slab: a flat piece of concrete that can form the basis of a foundation or a floor.

WORDS TO KNOW

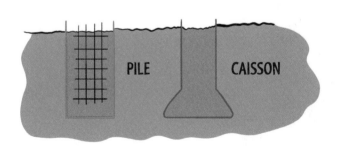

PILE   CAISSON

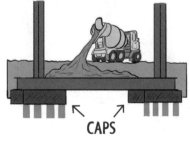

CAPS

WORDS TO KNOW

formwork: a set of molds into which concrete is poured during construction.

utilities: electricity, gas, water, cable, and telephone service in a building or house.

conduit: a channel through which electricity or water travels.

duct: a channel through which air, water, or cables can pass.

DID YOU KNOW?

Sometimes, there's a bottleneck when building a skyscraper! That means that all the construction on a building comes to a halt because of one problem.

GOING UP!

Once the foundation is complete, work on the floors begins. Formwork is built over structural columns. Pieces of rebar are placed where concrete will be poured. Then, utilities such as electricity and water must be routed through conduits and ducts. Concrete is poured to form a slab at the bottom of each floor and to fill the formwork.

As the floors get built, it can be more and more difficult to bring up all the needed equipment. To pump concrete up to higher floors, you need a powerful pump and a very long boom. A boom is a mechanical arm that controls where the concrete is poured.

Sometimes, construction workers get supplies up high by building a platform in the elevator shaft to go up and down as new floors get built. Not only can this platform bring up construction materials, it can also bring up supplies for the crew, such as microwaves, bathrooms, and snacks! Why is this important?

MOVING INSIDE

Once the last floor is built and all the windows are installed, it is time to frame the walls. First, plumbers and electricians run the rest of the wires and pipes that are needed for electricity and plumbing. Then, workers hang drywall to make the surface of the walls. Next, this drywall is sanded and painted. Floors are finished. Carpenters might work on shelving and cabinetry.

FROM THE TOP DOWN!

While most construction begins with the foundation, some big projects use a top-down process when they need to be completed quickly. Construction happens above and below the ground at the same time! Some teams of builders work on the **superstructure** above the ground and others work on digging out the basement levels below.

You can watch a video showing the top-down construction process at this website.

KEYWORD PROMPTS

ParkView Condo top down 🔍

This is the time when small mistakes are fixed. For example, if the floors are not perfectly level, workers can come in to fill and sand down the floors. It is important that everything is as perfect as it can be.

DID YOU KNOW?

In very big skyscrapers, sometimes shops are built into a self-rising platform so the crew rarely has to come down!

Construction ends when a certificate of occupancy is granted. A certificate of occupancy means the structure has been inspected and found safe. Then, yet another time-consuming process begins—renting or selling space in the skyscraper!

A skyscraper is a beautiful example of what human innovation and hard work can accomplish. In the next chapter, we'll take a look at some of the most impressive examples of skyscrapers around the world!

? CONSIDER AND DISCUSS

It's time to consider and discuss: Why does it take such strong teamwork to build a skyscraper?

CITY PLANNING

Cities do not develop without planning. Usually, many rules tell developers, architects, and builders how to build in a populated place. These regulations are meant to make a city a healthy and safe place for people to live in.

1 What do you think makes a good city or town? What must every city or town have? Do some brainstorming and write your answers down.

2 Use Google Earth to focus in on your city, town, or the closest city or town to you. How is the city laid out from a bird's-eye view? What do you notice about the layout? Why do you think it was developed in this way? Write your answers in your notebook.

3 Now, it's time to build. Your cardboard boxes will be buildings— use markers to label what kind of buildings they are and to draw windows and other architectural details. Lay the cardstock on the floor, add the buildings with tape, and draw in the streets.

4 What were the challenges you found in building your city? What does your city lack that it needs? Do you think people would be happy to live in your city? Why or why not? Reflect on these answers in your notebook.

THINK MORE: With an adult, look up the zoning regulations in your city or town. Are there rules about what kinds of buildings can be built where? Do you think these laws can be improved in any way? How?

JIGGLY GELATIN

How do engineers design buildings that will survive in an area that has a lot of earthquakes? In this project, you will build structures with marshmallows and toothpicks and then place them on a pan filled with gelatin. If you shake this jiggly gelatin, it will mimic the forces of an earthquake. See which of your structures is left standing by the end!

Caution: Have an adult help with cooking.

1 Make the gelatin in a long and shallow pan according to the recipe on the box. Allow time for it to cool in the refrigerator.

2 While you are waiting for the gelatin to thicken, start to build different structures using marshmallows and toothpicks. You can build them any way you want, but make sure they are at least 2 inches tall. You need between four and six different structures.

3 With an adult's permission, look up earthquakes online. What causes earthquakes? What damage can they do? Record your research in your notebook.

4 Place one structure at a time on the gelatin in the pan. Shake the pan to simulate an earthquake. Which structure remains standing? Why?

THINK MORE: Reflect on your experiment. What can engineers do to prevent buildings from falling down in earthquakes?

PROJECT!

INTERESTING INSULATION

SUPPLIES

* ✳ engineering notebook and pencil
* ✳ ice cubes
* ✳ plastic paper cups
* ✳ timer
* ✳ measuring spoons
* ✳ insulating materials, such as cotton balls, Styrofoam cups, newspaper, aluminum foil, plastic wrap, and fabric
* ✳ duct tape
* ✳ scissors

Building a skyscraper isn't just about constructing a tall tower. It also involves making that tower comfortable for the people inside. This can be very hard in terms of the temperature. In order to make a skyscraper livable, mechanical engineers need to design a way to insulate the skyscraper to keep it comfortable in the winter and summer.

1 Think about the word *insulation*. What does it mean? Why is it important to engineers? Write your answers in your notebook.

2 Place an ice cube in a plastic cup. Let it sit for 5 minutes. At the end of 5 minutes, pour out the liquid into measuring spoons and record the amount of liquid that has melted.

3 Use insulating materials to build an "ice chamber." Using tape, experiment with wrapping different materials around your cups. Build a few different ice chambers. Make sure that your ice cubes are kept frozen in the freezer as you build.

4 Repeat step 2 for each of your ice chambers. Which ice chamber was the best insulator? Why? Write your answers in your notebook.

THINK ABOUT IT: How does this experiment relate to skyscraper design? What kinds of materials should engineers use to insulate skyscrapers? Why?

WORDS TO KNOW

insulate: to keep the heat in and the cold out.

PROJECT!

MIMICKING MODELS

Visit the 3-D model warehouse at SketchUp, a free computer modeling program, at this website. In the search box, you can search for skyscrapers and find models of imaginary skyscrapers and copies of real ones!

KEYWORD PROMPTS

SketchUp 🔍

1 In SketchUp, choose a skyscraper model that you find especially interesting. Study that model.

2 Answer the following questions in your notebook.

* Is the design realistic to you?

* Is the model based on a real skyscraper? If not, do you think this skyscraper would work in the real world? Why or why not?

* What are some of the design elements you notice in this model, such as setbacks?

3 Design your own skyscraper. You can sketch it out in your engineering notebook or use SketchUp to build a model.

THINK ABOUT IT: What design elements did you use in your own skyscraper? Would it work better in some ways than the model you saw? Why or why not? How could you improve your design? Write your ideas in your notebook.

CHAPTER FIVE

FAMOUS SKYSCRAPERS

We live in an age of skyscrapers! Teams of architects and engineers are working every day to build taller and more impressive skyscrapers. Not only do people like to meet new challenges, we also need the living space as the world's population grows larger and larger.

Let's take a look at some of the most impressive modern skyscrapers around the world today. What do these buildings have in common? How are they different?

 INVESTIGATE!

What kind of skyscraper design would you like to see in the future? What purpose would this new design serve?

terrorist: someone who causes panic and anxiety as a way of controlling people.

economic: having to do with the resources and wealth of a country.

WORDS ⊙ KNOW

ONE WORLD TRADE CENTER

One World Trade Center, also known as the Freedom Tower, was built on the site of the former World Trade Centers in downtown Manhattan, New York. The World Trade Center Towers were destroyed on September 11, 2001, in a terrorist attack that claimed the lives of 2,977 people. These twin buildings were considered a symbol of the United States' economic power.

In 2002, one year after the buildings were destroyed, the City of New York organized a competition for ideas on how to develop the site. People wanted the new building to be both safe and beautiful. The famous architect Daniel Libeskind (1946–) submitted the design that was selected as the winner.

In May 2006, after many years of working on the design to make sure the tower would be safe, ground was broken and the construction team arrived to begin work. After using explosives to clear the site, 400 cubic yards of concrete were poured to form the skyscraper's foundation.

DID YOU KNOW?

One World Trade Center is one of the safest commercial buildings in the world. It has a center core that contains stairwells, elevators, gas and water lines, communication systems, emergency items, and a special elevator for firefighters.

ONE WORLD TRADE CENTER

It took many years to finish construction on this new skyscraper. Throughout 2010, one floor per week was constructed. By April 2012, the new building had become the tallest building in New York City, soaring past the Empire State Building at 1,250 feet. And it wasn't even finished yet!

One World Trade Center officially opened on November 3, 2014. It stands at 1,776 feet tall—the year the U.S. Declaration of Independence was signed. The skyscraper offers 69 floors of office space aboveground and 55,000 square feet of retail space underground, with connections to 11 subways as well as the ferry service.

This skyscraper also contains 40,000 metric tons of steel and is designed to be the safest office building in the world. It uses high-strength concrete reinforced with extra-long steel bars that can withstand much more pressure than regular concrete.

THE BURJ KHALIFA

The tallest structure in the world (as of the printing of this book) is the Burj Khalifa in Dubai, in the United Arab Emirates. A megatall skyscraper, the Burj Khalifa was completed in 2010 at a cost of $1.5 billion.

This skyscraper holds 900 apartments, 304 hotel rooms, 58 elevators, and a whopping 2,957 parking spaces! Its full height is 2,722 feet, with 1,918 feet of the tower occupied by hotel rooms and apartments.

CLEAN AIR

Vertical forest skyscrapers are being built all around the world, particularly in cities with lots of people and lots of pollution. Architect Stefano Boeri (1956–) first built vertical forest skyscrapers in Milan, Italy, in 2014. They were a huge success, not just because of the greenery they brought to the city but because of the way the trees filter out **carbon dioxide** from the air and emit **oxygen**. In 2018, Boeri completed the first vertical forest skyscrapers in Nanjing, China. These skyscrapers contain more than 1,100 trees and 2,500 other plants to improve air quality.

You can read more about Boeri's projects and see drawings of the design at this website.

KEYWORD PROMPTS

Stefano Boeri vertical 🔍

To build such a large structure, architects and engineers had to rethink their materials as well as the rules of building. The tower's plan features many setbacks to help it remain stable. These setbacks also help with wind force, which engineers tested on models of the Burj Khalifa before they began to build. The outside of the skyscraper was built with aluminum and stainless steel, which are both materials that can withstand the extremely hot temperatures of Dubai's summers.

The Burj Khalifa is so tall that it doesn't even need regular air conditioning on its higher floors. The air up there is much cooler than the air closer to the ground. This is called sky-sourced fresh air—air enters the building from the top and provides air conditioning and ventilation for the whole building.

WHAT IS AS BIG AS A SKYSCRAPER BUT WEIGHS NOTHING

HA HA HA

It's shadow!

THE PETRONAS TOWERS

The Petronas Towers in Kuala Lumpur, Malaysia, were the tallest buildings in the world from 1998 until 2004. They remain the tallest twin towers in the world as of the printing of this book. At 1,483 feet, the towers were named after Petronas, the national oil company of Malaysia. They were designed by the Argentinian architect Cesar Pelli (1926–).

According to the Malaysian government, while it did not set out to build the tallest towers in the world, it wanted to design a tall structure to show Malaysia's influence in the world, as well as its cultural heritage. The skyscraper features Islamic design, including an eight-point star formed by intersecting squares. The towers are linked by a bridge at the 41st floor, making the towers appear almost like a gateway to the capital city of Kuala Lumpur.

The tower is built with high-strength concrete to help with wind force. However, as we learned, concrete is heavier than steel. The foundation had to be very strong.

First, the building site was moved from an area that was half limestone and half soft rock to an area that was all soft rock. Then, engineers dug down hundreds of feet, creating the world's deepest foundation. Construction workers poured 470,000 cubic feet of concrete for each tower. Finally, engineers used a framed tube design to build the skyscraper.

JEDDAH TOWER

Soon, the Burj Khalifa will be the second-tallest tower in the world, only seven years after its completion. Newer and taller towers are being designed and built every few years!

The Jeddah Tower is being built in the port city of Jeddah in Saudi Arabia. When it's completed in 2019, the tower will reach 3,280 feet and be the first skyscraper ever built to reach the 1-kilometer mark.

THE BURJ KHALIFA

Designed by the American firm Adrian Smith + Gordon Gill Architecture, the 170-story building will house 439 apartments, 200 hotel rooms, and 65 elevators. Originally announced in 2011, the developer thought it would take about three years to complete the building once construction began. The foundation was poured in 2014. However, construction was delayed when the price of oil dropped, which caused Saudi Arabia to experience a shortage of money for large building projects such as the Jeddah Tower. While the original cost was estimated to be $1.2 billion, delays have pushed the total cost to at least $2 billion.

The Jeddah Tower will feature a triangular footprint to reduce wind loads. A sky terrace, the highest observatory in the world, will be on the 157th floor. It will have an air deck where visitors will be able to walk around in open air thousands of feet above the ground. Does that sound fun to you?

Just 100 years ago, many engineers and architects would never have imagined such tall and complex structures as the Burj Khalifa. Now, these structures have become almost the norm. Every year, another determined team of developers, architects, engineers, and builders pushes the limits to build taller and more innovative structures. Who knows what they will dream up—and build—next!

CONSIDER AND DISCUSS

It's time to consider and discuss: What kind of skyscraper design would you like to see in the future? What purpose would this new design serve?

THE LONGEST SKYSCRAPER

In New York, a skyscraper was recently proposed that would be the "longest skyscraper in the world." Why longest and not tallest? Because it would be in the shape of a giant upside-down U and would extend 4,000 feet from end to end! Known as the Big Bend, this horseshoe-shaped skyscraper would use horizontal elevators to transport visitors and residents. In the future, skyscrapers will be built in many ways to make the best use of space in our increasingly crowded cities.

PROJECT!

WOOD VS. STEEL

SUPPLIES

✻ computer with an internet connection
✻ engineering notebook and pencil

Some new architects are turning from steel-based to wood-based skyscraper designs. Why?

1 With an adult, read and discuss the World Economic Forum article found here called "The Skyscrapers of the Future Could Be Made of Wood."

KEYWORD PROMPTS

skyscrapers future wood 🔍

2 What are some reasons the article gives for why wood might be a better material to use for skyscrapers than steel and concrete? Write your answers in your notebook.

3 Now, think about the drawbacks of wood. Why has wood not been used to build skyscrapers before? Write these negatives in your notebook.

4 How could architects and engineers overcome these negatives? What new technologies exist to help make wood construction better?

EXPLORE MORE: Explore other proposed wooden skyscraper projects around the world. Look at the proposed River Beech project in Chicago, which would be a tower in the center of the city made out of high-tech wood. And Framework is a project for developing a wooden tower in Portland, Oregon. Which project is most likely to be completed? Which project seems the most interesting to you? Why?

UPHILL CLIMB

SUPPLIES

* 2 clear cups
* plastic container
* water
* clear, flexible tubing
* food coloring

Skyscrapers of the future may include gardens and greenery not only on the top floors but also on the outside walls. This makes skyscrapers more sustainable **and pretty, and can also make the air cleaner in big cities. However, moving water up to the top of skyscrapers is no easy task. Try it yourself by building a** siphon.

1 Fill one cup about two-thirds with water. Fill the second cup only half full with water.

2 Put the plastic container upside down on a table. Place the cup with more water on top. Place the second cup on the table several inches away. The first cup should be at least 4 inches above the second cup. Add food coloring to the water in the high cup.

3 Fill the clear tube with water. Block off the ends with your thumbs so that the water stays inside.

4 Put one end of the tube in the upper cup so that it is under water. Make sure that it stays underwater while you lift the center part of the tube so it forms a hill. Put the other end of the tube in the lower cup and release your thumb. This end of the tube does not need to be under water.

WORDS ᴛᴏ KNOW

sustainable: a process or resource that can be used without being completely used up or destroyed.

siphon: a tube that directs water to flow a certain way.

PROJECT!

5 Watch as the water from the top cup moves up the tubing before emptying out into the lower container. You can see the water move through the tubing with the food dye in it.

6 How did the water move up the tube in this experiment? Write your hypothesis in your notebook.

EXPLORE MORE: Read more about how siphons work at this website. How does your hypothesis compare to how siphons really work?

↓

KEYWORD PROMPTS
wonderopolis siphon 🔍

SUSTAINABLE SKYSCRAPERS

Sustainability is the balance between what's healthy for the environment and the use of natural resources for development. In this project, you will brainstorm different ways to make skyscrapers more sustainable. Maybe your ideas will create the skyscraper of the future!

1 Think of sustainable building materials. These are materials that can be used without hurting the environment, such as wood, straw, and dirt. Write more examples in your notebook. Why are they sustainable?

2 How might you build a skyscraper that is not only built out of sustainable materials but has a sustainable purpose? Brainstorm your ideas in your notebook.

3 Sketch a sustainable skyscraper. You can use colored pencils to make it look realistic. Write a one-paragraph summary of your skyscraper and what it does in your engineering notebook.

4 After designing your skyscraper, read about another sustainable skyscraper on this website. Do you think that these kinds of buildings are the way of the future? Why or why not?

↓

KEYWORD PROMPTS

skyscraper feed town 🔍

accessible: able to be entered.

acoustical engineer: an engineer who works with sound and the way sound travels through spaces.

architect: a person who designs buildings.

BCE: put after a date, BCE stands for Before Common Era and counts years down to zero. CE stands for Common Era and counts years up from zero. This book was published in 2018 CE.

beam: a rigid, horizontal structure that carries the load, or the weight.

borehole: a deep and narrow hole drilled into the ground to study the soil or to locate water.

brittle: easily broken, cracked, or snapped.

buckle: to collapse in the middle.

caisson: a hollow, waterproof structure that can be filled with cement to form the basis of foundations.

cantilever: a long beam that is fixed to a building or structure at only one end.

carbon dioxide: a colorless, odorless gas. It forms when animals breathe and when plants and other living matter die and rot.

civil engineer: an engineer who designs structures such as buildings, roads, bridges, and tunnels.

column: a vertical support structure.

complementary: forces that work together.

compression: a pushing force that squeezes or presses material inward.

computer-aided design (CAD): software used to create two-dimensional and three-dimensional drawings.

concrete: a hard construction material made with cement, sand, and water.

concrete slab: a flat piece of concrete that can form the basis of a foundation or a floor.

conduit: a channel through which electricity or water travels.

coordination: the organization of different parts working together.

counteract: to use an opposite force or action to work against something.

counterweight: a weight that balances another weight.

dead load: the weight of a building, excluding the weight of people, furniture, and goods inside it.

defy: to challenge or resist.

demolish: to tear down.

displacement: when something is moved by an object taking its place.

dominance: power and influence over others.

drywall: a building material that is used to form interior walls and ceilings in buildings.

duct: a channel through which air, water, or cables can pass.

ductile: bendable without breaking.

earthquake: a sudden movement in the outer layer of the earth.

economic: having to do with the resources and wealth of a country.

efficient: wasting as little as possible.

GLOSSARY

energy: the ability or power to do things, to work.

engineer: a person who uses science, math, and creativity to design and build things such as roads, bridges, and buildings.

engineering: the work an engineer does, using science and math to design and build things.

engineering design: the process engineers use to identify problems and come up with solutions.

feat: a product of skill or endurance.

flexible: capable of being bent or twisted without breaking.

footprint: in architecture, the amount of ground covered by a building.

force: a push or pull applied to an object.

formwork: a set of molds into which concrete is poured during construction.

foundation: the part of a building below the ground.

fragile: easily broken.

frame: a rigid structure that supports something.

framed tube: a type of frame used in skyscrapers to distribute and decrease weight loads.

geotechnical engineer: someone who studies, designs, and constructs foundations and other systems that are supported by soil or rock.

gravity: a force that pulls all objects toward the earth.

ground area: the area of a building, which is calculated using its exterior measurements. Also called the footprint.

heritage: the art, buildings, traditions, and beliefs that are important to a country's or the world's history.

high-rise: a building with many stories and with elevators, typically used for housing or offices.

horizontal: going straight across from side to side.

I-beam: a metal beam that looks like an I and is used to support weight in construction.

Industrial Revolution: a period of time beginning in the late 1700s when people started using machines to make things in large factories.

innovation: a new creation or a unique solution to a problem.

insulate: to keep the heat in and the cold out.

Islam: a religion developed in the Middle East that follows the teachings of the prophet Muhammad.

lateral force: a force applied to the sides of an object.

live load: the weight of people, furniture, and goods in a building.

load-bearing: supporting the weight of a structure.

mass: the amount of material that an object contains.

matter: anything that has weight and takes up space.

mechanical engineer: an engineer who designs and improves mechanical systems, such as elevators.

megatall: a skyscraper that is more than 1,969 feet tall.

84

Mesopotamia: a region of the Middle East that today is part of Iraq.

model: a miniature, three-dimensional representation of something to be constructed.

natural disaster: a natural event, such as a fire or flood, that causes great damage.

oxygen: a gas in the air that people and animals need to breathe to stay alive.

parallel: anything that is always the same distance away from something else.

permit: an official document that allows you to do something, such as put up a building.

physics: the science of how matter and energy work together. Matter is what an object is made of. Energy is the ability to perform work.

pile cap: a thick layer of concrete that rests on piles that were driven into the ground to form a stable foundation.

piles: heavy posts that are driven into the soil to support foundations.

predecessor: people, events, or things that came before.

project coordination: the organization of all steps required to complete a building project.

prototype: a model of something that allows engineers to test their ideas.

public health engineer: an engineer who designs and improves systems that are essential to human health, such as water systems.

pyramid: a large stone structure with a square base and triangular sides.

rebar: steel bars that are put into concrete to make it stronger.

recession: a part of a structure or wall that goes in from the main part.

riveted: connected with metal bolts, called rivets.

setback: a flat offset in a wall.

shake table: a platform that simulates the shaking caused by an earthquake.

shear: a sliding force that slips parts of a material in opposite directions.

shear wall: a paneled wall that is used to distribute weight in heavy buildings.

siphon: a tube that directs water to flow a certain way.

skeleton: a supporting frame.

skyline: an outline of land and buildings against the sky.

skyscraper: an extremely tall building.

soil core: a sample of soil to examine and test, shaped like the tube that was used to remove it.

stable: firmly established and not likely to change or move.

steel: a hard, strong material made of iron combined with carbon and other elements.

structure: something that is built, such as a building, bridge, tunnel, tower, or dam.

superstructure: a structure built on top of another structure.

supertall: a skyscraper that is more than 984 feet tall.

surpass: to be greater than something that came before.

sustainable: a process or resource that can be used without being completely used up or destroyed.

sway: the distance that a building can move from side to side.

technology: the tools, methods, and systems used to solve a problem or do work.

tension: a pulling force that pulls or stretches an object.

terrorist: someone who causes panic and anxiety as a way of controlling people.

three-dimensional (3-D): an image that has length, width, and height, and is raised off the flat page.

tomb: a room or place where a dead person is buried.

torsion: a twisting force.

truss: a network of beams and bars that relies on triangles to support a load.

utilities: electricity, gas, water, cable, and telephone service in a building or house.

vertical: up and down.

x-bracing: diagonal support beams that intersect to provide more stability for a structure.

ziggurat: a stepped tower with a temple on top.

zoning: the division of a city into different sections that can be used for different purposes, such as business or residence.

METRIC CONVERSIONS

Use this chart to find the metric equivalents to the English measurements in this book. If you need to know a half measurement, divide by two. If you need to know twice the measurement, multiply by two. How do you find a quarter measurement? How do you find three times the measurement?

English	Metric
1 inch	2.5 centimeters
1 foot	30.5 centimeters
1 yard	0.9 meter
1 mile	1.6 kilometers
1 pound	0.5 kilogram
1 teaspoon	5 milliliters
1 tablespoon	15 milliliters
1 cup	237 milliliters

BOOKS

Bernhardt, Carolyn. *Engineer It! Skyscraper Projects.*
Super Sandcastle, 2018

Romero, Libby. *National Geographic Skyscrapers.*
National Geographic, 2017

Burns, Kylie. *A Skyscraper Reaches Up.*
Crabtree Publishing Company, 2017

Hardyman, Robyn. *Skyscrapers.*
Powerkids Press, 2017

Loh-Hagan Edd, Virginia. *Skyscrapers.*
Cherry Lake Publishing, 2017

Latham, Donna. *Skyscrapers: Investigate Feats of Engineering.*
Nomad Press, 2013

WEBSITES

National Geographic: Building the Skyscraper
youtube.com/watch?v=QSG7DtaAeQ0

Constructing a Skyscraper
youtube.com/watch?v=K4oj95E8J9M

SciShow: How Tall Can Skyscrapers Get?
youtube.com/watch?v=Cioj_KYMVP8

Popular Mechanics for Kids: Buildings
youtube.com/watch?v=azlKa4O6VDk

World's Most Amazing Places and Photos: Skyscrapers
youtube.com/watch?v=79Zhyl_A3hU

SketchUp
sketchup.com

QR CODE GLOSSARY

Page 11: youtube.com/watch?v=MZn0OakXvlc

Page 22: pbskids.org/zoom/activities/sci/newspaperchair.html#results

Page 29: theguardian.com/world/video/2015/apr/30/
china-build-57-storey-skyscraper-19-days-timelapse-video

Page 31: sketchup.com

Page 37: commons.wikimedia.org/wiki/File:Lighthouse_-_Thiersch.png

Page 58: youtube.com/watch?v=_OwOaaZUbGQ&feature=youtu.be

Page 65: youtube.com/watch?v=AgaAedBl5K8

Page 70: 3dwarehouse.sketchup.com

Page 74: dezeen.com/2014/05/15/
stefano-boeri-bosco-verticale-vertical-forest-milan-skyscrapers

Page 79: weforum.org/agenda/2017/06/timber-skyscrapers-of-the-future

Page 81: wonderopolis.org/wonder/how-does-a-siphon-work

Page 82: weforum.org/agenda/2017/04/
this-futuristic-vertical-farm-could-feed-an-entire-african-town

INDEX

INDEX